Richard Cromwell. Lord Protector 3 September 1658 – 25 May 1659:

4,200 words

Amazon Kindle October 2022

Contents:

Images:

Image 1 (cover photo) - Potrait of Richard Cromwell.

Image 2 - Image of Huntington. Oliver Cromwell's birthplace.
www.artuk.co.uk

Image 3 - Oliver Cromwell alongside John Lambert. Studio of Robert Walker

Image 4 - Image of Charles II. Painting by Peter Lely (1630 - 1685). Royal Museums Greenwich

Timeline of events:

1626 4th October: Richard Cromwell is born at Huntington

1649 Richard marries Dorothy Maijor

1649 28th June: Oliver Cromwell appointed Lord General and commander-in-chief of parliament's forces

1649 30th June: King Charles I is executed in Whitehall

1653 16th December: Oliver Cromwell Inaugrated as Lord Protector of Britain and Ireland

1654 Spring: Oliver Cromwell and his family take up residence at Whitehall Palace and Hampton Court

1658 3rd September: Dies at Whitehall. Suceeded as Protector by his eldest son Richard

1658 23th November: State funeral of Oliver Cromwell

1659 January: Parliament approves Richard as Lord Protector

1659 25th May: Coup against Richard Cromwell who is removed from power by the Army

1660 Spring: The restoration of the monarchy and Charles II

1712 12th July: Richard Cromwell dies at Cheshunt

Key figures:

Oliver Cromwell - Lord Protector of Great Britian and Ireland 1653-1658

Richard Cromwell - Eldest son of Oliver Cromwell. Would suceed his father as Lord Protector in 1658

Henry Cromwell - Fourth son of Oliver Cromwell. Was ruler of Ireland on behalf of Great Britian from 1657-1659. Criticised for his rule in Ireland

Charles Fleetwood - Led the military in the civial war. Married the daughter of Oliver Cromwell. Governor of Ireland and would lead the military coup against Richard in 1659

George Monck (1st Duke of Albemarle) - Became General of the New Model Army and was Army General during the period between the resignation of Richard Cromwell and Charles II accesion

John Lambert - Gained the title 'Major General'. Would become Deputy Lord Leiutenant of Ireland. Key military figure in the civil wars and during the Protectorate

Introduction:

This study will analyse the eight months that preceeded Oliver Cromwell's death and the removal of his son Richard and the end of the Protectorate. An act that would lead to the restoration of the monarchy and the coronation of King Charles II. Using primary sources and academic analysis this study will seek to ask wether the fall of Richard Cromwell's regime was inevitable? How popular was Oliver Cromwell by the time of his death. Was he still supported by his Council and the key military figures who were alongside him since the civil war.

We all know the story of the origins of the English Civil War, the execution of Charles I. The puritan regime of Oliver Cromwell that gained power soon after, this would lead to him gained supreme power on a par to Charles I. Once he died, Charles II the son of the executed King rode back into London. He was offered the crown and in 1660 the monarchy was restored and the brief experiment of republican rule was ended. This version of events fits well into a history that follows a straight line and works well for historians with centuries of heinsight. This study will seek to deal with the final part of the story - what happened after Oliver Cromwell died.

The mid 1650's Oliver Cromwell was at the peak of his political career. He has become Lord Protector by 1653. A title that would make him equal to King Charles I. Head of State and Commander in Chief of the military. His family now live at Whitehall. With echoes of past monarchs Oliver had in the previous years even started military expiditions into Ireland, these though were at best mixed. The 1649 massacre of Drogheda which saw 3,500 people die is rightly something that . By 1657 Oliver's fourth son Henry would be put in charge of British affairs in Ireland after previously serving as military exploits in the Kingdom. Charles Fleetwood would serve under Henry. Through out all of these years, there is virtually no mention of Richard, Oliver's eldest son. Even the appointment as Justice of the Peace in Hampshire didn't end well. 'Unlike his younger brother Henry, Richard was not appointed to the Nominated Assembly in July 1653 nor to public office when his father was named Lord Protector the following December'. (http://bcw-project.org). During Oliver's final years, Richard played a very small part at Court and in Parliamentary sessions. He was certainly not positioned as his appointed heir as medieval monarchs would with their own succesors. It is hard to understand or explain Oliver's actions here, whether history would have gone a different way if another member of the Cromwell family or Fleetwood had indeed succeeded him is tough to know. What ever the difference, Richard was played a tough hand with a Parliament that at the very least were anxious over his lack of experience.

On 3rd September in 1658 in Whitehall Oliver Cromwell passed away at the age of 59. At this time the son of Charles I was on the European mainland struggling to be remembered and failing in every attempt to gain support for an 'invasion' of England. As Charles Miller notes 'Through 1657 and 1658 the prospects for Charles restoration were no brighter. Glimmers of hope were quickly extinguished. Spanish invasion plans were thwarted by an English naval blockade; Cromwell's death did not lead to the collapse of the Protectorate' (Miller:14). Oliver was succeeded by his eldest son Richard soon after his death. His regime quickly collapsed, due to a military junta and a wish for greater power. Crucially for a period of time after Richard's removal, parliamentary forces led by Fleetwood would attempt to call a new parliament amid widespread call for an end of military rule. Months of tussle between the Rump and the Army resulted in March 1660 an new assembly being set up with the House of Commons and House of Lords in attendance, all sides agreed to the need for a constitutional parlimantary system. Charles II's agreement to this and his coronation would start the road towards the parliamentary consitiuion we have still to this day, with the monarchy holding consititutional but not political control.

I will argue that the road to the restoration of the monarchy and Charles II as King was not inevitable. Richard's rise to the Protectorate was not doomed from the start but a lack of understanding of the military and the financial situaion gave him a tough hand and task to keep everything under control. The real power brokers near the end of Oliver Cromwel's reign and all of Richard's short reign was the military leaders. His decision to support a ill-timed civilan attack on the army in the spring of 1569 showed the desperate state he had become and the coup there after was inevitable. Charles II wasn't particularly a popular figure awaiting a return, he was arguably the best option after the failure of republican government after Richard's fall.

Image 2 - Death mask of Oliver Cromwell. National Trust Collections.

Chapter 1 - Oliver Cromwell's death:

1658 started the year with a new parliament being opened by Oliver Cromwell to reistablish his authority and control of events. 'When parliament met again in January 1658 the hitherto excluded members were admitted on taking an oath to be faithful to the Protector. In consequence opponents of the constitution captured control of the Commons, and in February Cromwell dissolved Parliament. Seven months later he died' (H F Mains 115). What ever Cromwell had hoped would be achieved by the new Parliament it failed and only showed the problems he now faced.

In the summer of 1658 Oliver Cromwell, Lord Protector of Great Britain and Ireland was seriously ill. His health and grip on power within the military and parliament was starting to falter. At the age of 59 it was unclear if Oliver Cromwell would get better and the Petition and Advice legislation had authorised him to nominate a succesor, his eldest son Richard was named. It is unknown if Oliver saw his death as approaching or whether this was simply a parliamentary mechanism to ensure a smooth transfer of power if he got more ill. On the eve of his death, Cromwell had accepted his mortality, and the proximity of his end, he remarked to his cloests allies: 'I would be willing to live to be further serviceable to God and His people, but my work is done' Unfortunately for his country, it was left undone. The succesion question remained and the Protector's answer was a tentative one (Lay, 2020.). At the very least it was a rushed appointment, the lack of any official mechanism to have a named succesor in a republic. Similar to more recent transfers of power when the leader who overthrown the old regime suddenly dies, the succesor is not always accepted by the old guard who hold the belief and vision that the regime's goals are unfinished.

On Friday 3rd September Oliver Cromwell died at Whitehall during the mid-afternoon. The precise reasons why Cromwell died in 1658 have never proven. At the times there were a number of theory's that were discussed from he died of malaria, fever or that he was poisoned. It gives an indication of the mood in the country that the idea he could have been murdered are given support. At the time England was in financial downturn, trade with other countries had declined since the commonwealth was created. The very reason for why they supported the removal of Charles I was now being repeated. Oliver Cromwell was an unelected head of state who seemed to be more interested in consolidating power between a small group of family and parliamentary members. The fruits of the Commonwealth had been spent.

With support from primary sources and later studies we will analyse every theory:

The most controversial part of Cromwell's death was that he was poisioned. This has been supported since the autopsy was conducted by Bates. In a letter from the period Bates remarks, 'His Body being opened; in the Animal parts, the Vessels of the Brain seemed to be overcharged; in the Vitals the Lungs a little inflamed; but in the Natural, the source of the distemper appeared; the Spleen, though sound to the Eye, being within filled with matter like to the Lees of Oyl. Bates. letter

The poison theory has been argued most strongly by American Professor H F McMains, who argues that Cromwell was deliberately poisoned during summer 1658, initially with antimony, then during much of August with mercury, and then, when those failed to kill the intended victim, finished off with a massive dose of arsenic administered on 2 September ... the (deliberately?) vague and inconclusive nature of Bate's autopsy report, together with vague or strange passages in some contemporary accounts and inconsistencies between them. He concludes that the evidence points, not to death from malaria or other natural causes (though he concedes malaria may have been present near the end), but to a deliberate, well-planned and ultimately successful plot to murder Cromwell by poisoning him. He suggests that Cromwell was poisoned by Bate, assisted by Thomas Clarges and the future bishops of London and Worcester. (McMains, www.OliverCromwell.org.uk) It is hard nearly five centuries after the event to conclusively say whether the poisioning argument carries weight. The fact that the poisioning came from the hands of regligous leaders rather than the military gives an indication how far his regime had fallen since he led the Parliamentary forces in the decisive battles of the Civil War and would eventually give approval for state regicide of Charles I. The puritincal aspect of his regime which saw him publicly attack the bishops and religues leaders who served under Charles I. He opposed many customs of the Church of England, a religion that was dominant since Elizabeth I had gained the throne in the laste 1500's. Puritanism was seen as a radical and extreme religious sect who were more interested in destroying their rivals and promoting their faith absolutely.

It is more likely that Cromwell died from a recurring illness that had affected him for many years 'His illness of late 1649 while in Ireland marked the onset of the disease. Although he had just turned fifty and so was probably past his physical prime, he was then still strong and robust and so threw off this first visitation quite easily. Subsequent visitations, together with other afflictions during the 1650s – dysentery was reportedly present during his long illness in Edinburgh in 1651, boils and abscesses continued to cause trouble, and intermittent problems with kidney or bladder stones are indicated by some accounts – and the general decline caused by advancing years noted by the Venetian ambassador and others rendered Cromwell less able to throw off attacks as quickly or as easily and made him more vulnerable. Having fought a clearly sharp and vigorous attack for over a month during summer 1658, his fifty-nine year old body could continue the struggle no longer and the fifth bout of fever in early September quickly killed him. Malarial fever is the most likely and the most widely accepted explanation for Cromwell's death' (McMains, www.OliverCromwell.org.uk)

Image 3. Oliver Cromwell alongside John Lambert. Studio of Robert Walker

Soon after Oliver Cromwell's death, in line with the succession plans his eldest son Richard is appointed as his succesor and Lord Protector (Head of State). Richard was the least prepared sucessor in British history, whilst previous and subsequent leaders would be guided through the early years by an experienced family member and a Council of elders who would be willing to support the regime largely based on. Contemprary sources give us an idea of the public mood, those who read the offical proclamation in Oxford were 'pelted by some junior scholars... with turnip and carrot top... More significantly, there was clearly the kind of opposition which Henry Cromwell had predicted, from men who 'say they have better deserve to govern there than any of Cromwell's sons' and who felt that 'Henry Cromwell is fitter than Richard' (Little, 2008). There were sources supporting Richard's claim to be Protectorate, but these were mostly by people who supporting the idea of monarchical succession rather than the people who saw Richard's lack of experience. Image 3 a painting of Oliver Cromwell and his trusted ally John Lambert it is a good reference to remind us that Oliver's Protectorate was heavily dependent on military support and his own military record gave him prestige and cover that neither of his children had.

Chapter 2 - Richard's Protectorate:

Little over two months after Oliver Cormwells' funeral cortage rode through London, his on Richard was appointed as his succesor, in line with his father's wishes. Richard become head of state and head of the military. A heavy responsibility for any 32 year old, but especially one trying to deal with the collapsed and disparate regime of his father's final years. As Hill notes. Richard had none of his father's prestige with the Army. A Parliament (elected on the old franchise) met in January 1659 and recognised the new Protector. (Hill, 2002:115) the second sentence would be the most crucial. Unlike other ruler's Richard didn't have any allies or supporters who he could give influnetial positions to, as a way of rewarding their loyalty and protecting him from rival clamiants. He was heavily reliant from day one of his father's allies. Even before Oliver's death they were already becoming disillusioned with the the regime.

In all sense of purposes Richard was head of a military regime. It gave support to parliament if it gave assurances on peace, stability and a healthy economy that would steer the country away from the perils of the civil war years. Gaunt notes, Cromwell had done little to prepare Richard for office and bequeathed him acute financial problems and military tension which soon overwhelmed him (Gaunt, 2004: 134). Richard was starting his regime with one hand behind his back, not able to express himself or his views within the dire financial situation in the country.

His relationship with the army, a group he had barely communicated with before his promotion to Lord Protectorate did not improve. As Lay notes, he was comfortable with the regime's civilian faction, though he never impressed or ingratiated himself with the army radicals; Desborough in particular, despite his familial links, despised him (Lay, 2020). Unlike his brother Henry who had been in the military and fought alongisde them in campaigns in Ireland . Richard had poor results during his time in the military and seemed to be comfortable with being more of a civil servant. Unsuprisngly as soon as he became Protectorate, the leadership of the military were concerned if they would keep there power and if he wasn't the answer then what would the future hold for them.

This question would be answered very soon. With the economy bringing hard times for the populace and Parliament becoming increasingky sytarined by different power factions. Five months after being declared Lord Protector in the House of Commons, Richard was removed from the very men who kept his father in power. The risk to them of financial ruin, foreign enemies taking advantage of England's vunerability and there own machinations of government meant a military style government was the only option. Hill notes, a Cromwellian limited monarchy was impossible because Oliver was the creation of the Army and dared not disband it. No-one else could suceed where he failed, not Richard Cromwell, not Lambert or Fleetwood, not Monck. England plunged into anarchy (Hill. 2002: 136). The unrest of the army, in this new regime where they were expected to govern together and leave the civil unrest for the previous decade was hard to put into action.

One of the shortest 'reigns' that England had was now over. Crucially it would also mark the end of the Cromwell family's positon in society. Oliver Cromwell's achievement would be forgotten and greater focus on the mistakes of the past would become a byword of the next century. King Charles II would speed up there demise. Not suprisingly the Commonwealth of England i.e Republic would be known only for its corruption and rivarlys.

Chapter 3 - Charles II and the road to the Restoration:

The fascinating aspect of the 1650's and 1660's in England was that nothing as we now see with a historian hat on was to contemporaries inevitable or expected. Charles II didn't suceed Oliver Cromwell and he certainly didn't suceed Richard Cromwell. Once Richard's regime had collapsed, those who held the real levers of power, the military figures of Charles Fleetwood and George Monck who would become leader of the new Model Army attempted to keep this fractured country together. Miller gives an insight to the situation, In December 1659 the army succumbed to what would now be called 'people power'. As law enforcement and tax collection ground to a halt - it was claimed that judges were working - calls for a free Parliament became increasingly insistent. Some wanted fresh elections, other's Richards Parliament or the Long Parliament as it had been before Pride's purge, with a presbyterian majority. Londoners drew up a petition for a Parliament; the soldiers tried to suppress it and in the ensuing clashes at least two people were killed. Popular hatred of the army was taking its toll. (18 Charles II. Miller) For the military the tide was quickly turning against them as well. Similar to contemporary case studies. The military removing a unpopular regime would be praised but how quickly they transfered power to a democratic leader or in this case back to the Monarchy would decide how events would turn out.

As Gaunt notes. This would lead to a revivial of the Monarchy but also crucially for the first time give an understanding that one can't lead without the other. Over time this new balanced rule of Govenrment would become now as 'Constitutional Monarchy' and 'Parliamentary Government'; 'The collapse of Richard's Protectorate in spring 1569 led to a period of constitutional instability ending with the Restoration of the stuarts and traditional monarchical government in 1660, whereupon Charles reversed many of the policies of the preceeding years. (134. Gaunt) The New Model Army would be sumerged into the expanding British military and many of the tactics helped Britain to begin its imperial adventure over the next centuries.

Image 4 - Charles II. Peter Lely. Royal Museums Greenwich

The contradiction of a republic where the head of state was succeeded by his eldest son was a situation they could not recover from. A Cromwellian limited monarchy was impossible because Oliver was the creation of the Army and dared not disband it. No-one else could suceed where he failed, not Richard Cromwell, not Lambert or Fleetwood, not Monck. England plunged into anarchy. Two themes can be heard across the chaos... on the left, desperate pleas for reunion of republicans, democrats, and sectaries with the Army to defend the Good Old Cause. But the history of the past twelve years had split the radicals irretrievably. (136. Hill). The army had become too big and was problematic when attempting to run a country and to solve all of the problems that it faced espeically from its creditors and the reduction in trade with the continent.

Their gamble failed. They succeeded in removing Richard from power, but at the cost of losing control of the London crowd. The factional politics created by this political vacuum destabilised the government. In the uncertainty that followed – which seemed to many observers to threaten a third civil war – General Monck purged his Scottish army of republican radicals and began a long march south. Owen and other republicans wrote to ask his intentions, but his answers were ambiguous and evasive. What was clear was that the revolution was being unwound. Republican idealists had scuttled the government in the hope of renewing the ideals of the revolution. It was too much to hope for. (Gribben. 2018 www.historytoday.com)

Conclusion:

On a crisp morning on 30th June in 1649 the English people saw their Monarch executed for high treason. This ended years of civil war, death on both sides and suspension of Parliament. It was a dawn of a new age where anything was possible. A new England could be created on new ideals. Yet 11 years later, less than a generation King Charles I's son also named Charles would be asked back to the Kingdom to take charge. This is not only a victory for those who never forgive the regicide of the previous King but a massive failure for those who had hope for a new direction for England. This book has seeked to understand the timeline of this unique transition from monarch back to monarch through the brief reign of Richard Cromwell.

This study seeks to bring Richard Cromwell and his short time as Lord Protector out of the shadows and into the forefront of our historical conciousness. The collapse of English Republican in 1660 and the return of a monarchy, that has endured to this day is less about the positive aspects of (Second) Charles Stuart but the factions that developed under Oliver's reign that would eventually destroy his son. The Cromwell family's lack of historical lineage and prestige that any member of the royal family could show would also be their downfall. The decison to put Oliver's head in London for public view once the monarchy had been restored would enable the new regime to draw a clear line between the arguments of the Cromwellian regimes and the percieved stability of the Stuarts.

The military figures who helped to over throw Charles I, would be the same people who would ask his son to return. It is easy to argue if Oliver Cromwell had been succeeded by a military leader rather than a family member the republic would have lasted longer. But that answer is too simplistic. The whole apparatus of Government was becoming unpopular and becoming strained under the many competing aims of the regime. Let alone the bribery and corruption that was becoming common place. From Puritanism promoted throughout the Kingdom to the detriment and at times destruction of the Catholic faith. New purpose of the Model Army in relation to future conflicts. Crucially abject failures in Ireland and Scotland had taken the glosh off their reputation. Promotion of individuals of the Regicide to thank them for their work was hard to achieve whilst trying to balance the current structure. It was a delicate house of cards that was always going to end badly.

With Richard gone. Monck's intervention made possible the election of a new Parliament, the Convention Parliament, which, to no one's surprise, voted to recall the king. In May 1660, on his 30th birthday, Charles II marched into London. The English republic was over, undermined by its own political ends. (Gribben. 2018 www.historytoday.com)On May 1660 Charles II was proclaimed King of England. A year later he would be crowned King of England at Westminister Abbey. Aligning his reign with his father and all of the previous monarchs of England. With great spectacule his coronation was seen as the start of a great new era in English history where the last few decades of war between Parliament and the monarch would come to an end and the birth of constitutional monarchy would be begin. This would be joined by a commitment to blacken Oliver Cromwell's name - he would move his head to site on top of Tower Bridge for all of his supporters to see what happens to someone who threatens the King. At the same time all mention of Richard Cromwell would be virtually erased from history and to the peoples concisiouness. Historians know that this pr campaign wouldn't be totally sucessfull and the Stuart dynasty would face more challenges with parliament and religion.

Bibliography:

Secondary Sources:

Oliver Cromwell and the rule of the purtians in England. C H Firth. 2015

Providence lost: the rise & fall of Cromwell's Protectorate. Paul Lay. 2021

God's Englishman: Oliver Cromwell and the English Revolution. Christopher Hill. 1990

Stuart age: England, 1603-1714. Barry Coward. 2000

The Two Protectors: Oliver and Richard Cromwell. Tangye and Sir Richard. 2014

Protector: A life history of Richard Cromwell. Jane Ross Hammer. 1997

History of Richard Cromwell and the Restoration of Charles II. Andrew R Scoble. 2016

The Century of Revolution. Christopher Hill. 2002

Charles II. John Miller. 1991

Oliver Cromwell. Peter Gaunt. 2004

The death of Oliver Cromwell. H F McMains. 2014

The end of the English Republic. Crawford Gribben. www.historytoday.com 2018

Primary Sources:

Lansdowne collection of letters. British Museum. Vol 821. 153 and 154. Private letters between Richard Cromwell and his brother Henry

Letter wrote in 1652 to an unknown male friend. Cromwell Museum

Printed in Great Britain
by Amazon

47390845R00020